Volume 1

SAXOPHONE SOLOS
Bb Tenor with piano accompaniment
Editor: Paul Harvey

INDEX

CHESTER MUSIC

A division of Music Sales Ltd.
8/9 Frith Street, London, W1V 5TZ

EDITOR'S NOTES

1. **The Red Piper's Melody**
    A traditional Welsh folk song, which is ideal for developing the breath control necessary for this style of sustained melodic playing.

2. **The Swan**   Camille Saint-Saens (1835-1921)
    The well known cello solo from 'The Carnival of Animals'.

3. **Allegro from Suite XIV**   George Frederick Handel (1685-1759)
    The second movement from one of Handel's sixteen keyboard suites.

4. **Andaluza**   Enrique Granados (1867-1916)
    One of this composer's many piano pieces in Spanish nationalist idiom.

5. **"Love in Her Eyes Sits Playing"**   George Frederick Handel
                                                                    (1685-1759)
    A song from Handel's Serenata "Acis and Galatea", which he composed for the Duke of Chandos in 1720.

6. **Christopher's Caper**   Dorothy Harvey
    A lighthearted piece composed especially for this volume. The title possibly refers to the founder of the London Saxophone Quartet.

7 and 8. **Two Pieces for Tenor Saxophone and Piano**   Carey Blyton
    Saxe Blue (Op. 65c) A nostalgic evocation of the 1920's.
    Mock Joplin (Op. 69c) A parody of a music hall song, with a ragtime chorus.
    These two pieces are dedicated to the leading American exponent of the tenor saxophone, James Houlik, Professor of Saxophone at East Carolina University.

Paul Harvey. 1979.

1
The Red Piper's Melody

Welsh Traditional

CH55207

2
The Swan

Saint Saëns

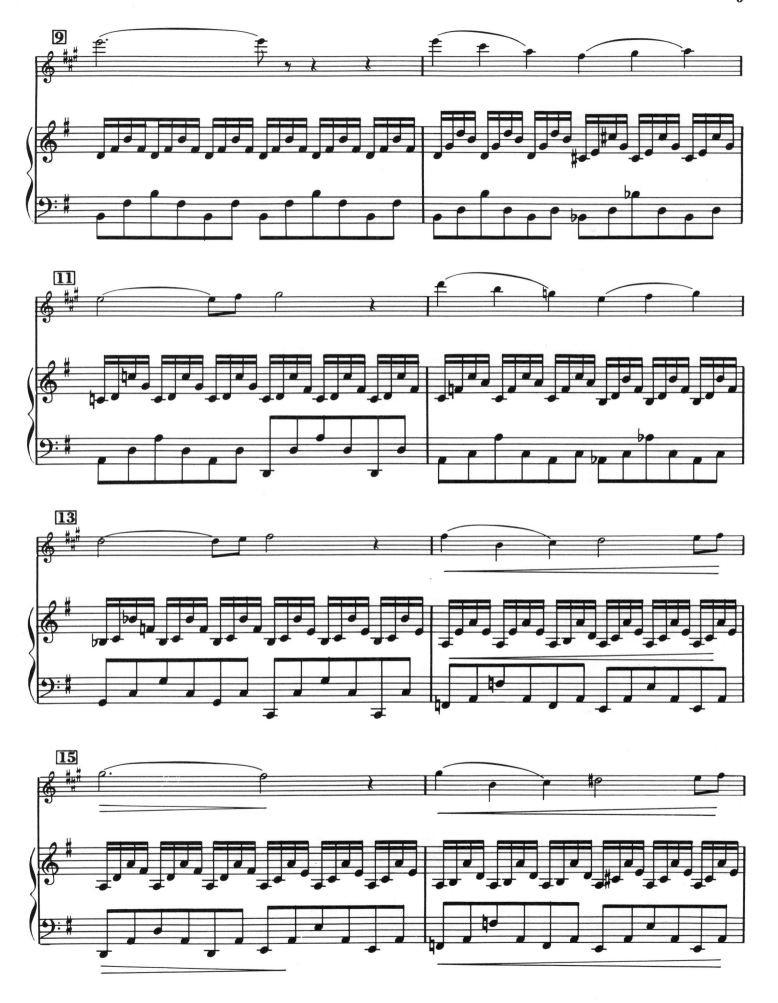

3
Allegro from Suite XIV

G. F. Handel

4
Andaluza

Granados

5.
Love in Her Eyes Sits Playing

Handel

6
Christopher's Caper

Dorothy Harvey

7
for James Houlik
Saxe Blue

"Half to remember days that have gone by ..." James Elroy Flecker, "Brumana"

Slow blues tempo ♩ = 66

Carey Blyton, Op. 65c

*2nd time only
Used by kind permission of Edizioni Musicali Bèrben.

8
for James Houlik
Mock Joplin

Carey Blyton, Op. 69c

Flute   Editor: Trevor Wye   Clarinet   Editor: Thea King

Oboe   Editor: James Brown   Bassoon   Editor: William Waterhouse

Saxophone   Editor: Paul Harvey

A growing collection of volumes from Chester Music, containing a
wide range of pieces from different periods.

E♭ ALTO SAXOPHONE VOLUME I

Bizet	L'Arlesienne
Mussorgsky	The Old Castle
	from "Pictures at an Exhibition"
Delibes	Barcarolle
	from "Sylvia"
Kodaly	The Battle and Defeat of Napoleon
	from "Hary Janos"
Greaves	What is Beauty but a Breath?
Byrd	Pavane for the Earl of Salisbury
D. Harvey	Lullaby for a Saxophone
C. Blyton	In Memoriam Scott Fitzgerald

E♭ ALTO SAXOPHONE VOLUME II

Vaughan Williams	Dance of Job's Comforters
Sullivan	"The Sun and I"
J. S. Bach	Menuet
J. S. Bach	Badinerie
Handel	Allegro
D. Harvey	London's Burning
C. Cowles	Tolmers Village
P. Harvey	Caprice Anglais

B♭ TENOR SAXOPHONE VOLUME I

Welsh Trad.	The Red Piper's Melody
Saint-Saens	The Swan
Handel	Allegro from Suite XIV
Granados	Andaluza
Handel	"Love in Her Eyes Sits Playing"
D. Harvey	Christopher's Caper
C. Blyton	Saxe Blue
C. Blyton	Mock Joplin

B♭ TENOR SAXOPHONE VOLUME II

Ravel	Bolero
H. Millars	Andante and Rondo
D. Harvey	Christopher's Calypso
C. Cowles	Three Sketches from Bala
P. Harvey	Rue Maurice-Berteaux
Fiocco	Arioso

Also available: SAXOPHONE QUARTETS

Further details on request

CHESTER MUSIC

A division of Music Sales Ltd.
8/9 Frith Street, London, W1V 5TZ

Exclusive distributors: Music Sales Ltd. Newmarket Road,
Bury St Edmunds, Suffolk, IP33 3YB.